PREMANJALI
Selected Love Poems

DR. C.V. RAVINDRANATH

Presentation by *BookLeaf Publishing*

Web: www.bookleafpub.com
E-mail: info@bookleafpub.com

ISBN: 9789369545384

First edition 2025

Happy Birthday!

Dear C V Ravindranath.

Wish you a very Happy Birthday
May this year bring more
happiness and success in your life!

Narendra Modi

ॐ MAHA TRIPURA SUNDARIYE NAMAH:

Curriculum Vitae of Dr. C.V. Ravindranath HMCT, PDSHM, MA, MPhil, PhD (Mgmt), PhD (Philo), D. Litt (SQ).

Vision and Mission Statement of DR. C.V. Ravindranath

VISION:	PURITY	•	CREATIVITY	•	SPIRITUALITY
MISSION:	WISDOM	•	WELLNESS	•	WEALTH
	(SARASWATI)		(PARVATI)		(LAXMI)

I BIRTH:

C.V. Ravindranath was born in Colombo to an affluent family of Jewellers, ISLAND GOLD HOUSE, which was recognized by Her Majesty Queen Elizabeth of England at that time. He is a virgoan born on 24th August 1954 at 9 pm – Punnartham Nakshathram (VIRGO); in Ratna Hospital, Colombo, Ceylon.

II ALUMNI:

1. St. Teresa's Anglo-Indian Convent – Kindergarten (Baby class) – 1960.

2. St.Michael's Anglo-Indian Boys' High School, Kannur- Anglo-Indian Schools Examination, Chennai (1961-1971) Madras Board of Anglo-Indian Examinations.

3. P.S.G College of Technology, Coimbatore – Pre-Technical (1972-1973).

4. Birla Institute of Technology and Science (BITS) Pilani, Rajasthan – 1st B Tech(Hons) - (1973-1974) (Discontinued due to extreme cold climate).

5. Institute of Hotel Management, Catering Technology and Applied Nutrition, Mumbai- HMCT, PDSHM (1976-1980).

6. Cornell University, School of Hotel Administration, USA – Hotel Sales & Marketing (1983).

7. Gemological Institute of America (GIA), USA – Fine Jewellery Sales Consultant (1991).

8. Indian Diamond Institute(IDI), Surat – Diamond – Sales (1992).

9. Indian Institute of Management (IIM), Ahmedabad – SMEP (2000).

10. Indian Institute of Kozhikode, MDP (2001).

11. Regional Engineering College & Management studies – MDP (2002).

12. Madurai Kamaraj University, Madurai – MA & MPhil (2004-2006).

13. Indian School of Business – (ISB) Hyderabad – MDP (2007).

14. Kannur University, Dept. of Philosophy, PhD – The Prospects of Meditative Techniques in Transforming Socio–Personal Domains of Fundamentalism (2008-2013).

15. International Open University, Colombo, Honorary PhD in SQ in Business Management (2014).

16. Academy for Spiritual Scientist – Kingship Academy: Honorary Doctorate in Spirituality (2015).

CONTENTS

PREFACE

In this collection of poems, Premanjali, Dr. C.V. Ravindranath invites readers into an introspective journey through the depth of human emotions, spirituality, and the beauty of nature. Each poem serves as a reflection on life's profound truths, touching on themes of love, solitude, fantasy, reality, and Universalism.

Through his poetic words, Dr. C.V. Ravindranath portrays the raw beauty of natural forces, relationship between the elements of nature and turn into a metaphor of boundless love and energy. He offers a gentle reminder of the inner light each individual carries, even in times of grief and speaks to the universal human experience, drawing strength and beauty from introspection and resilience.

In rhythmic lines he explores the world of desire, the celebration of beauty, and the splendor found in simple gestures and emotions.

This collection is more than a journey through poetic landscapes; it is an invitation to reflect on the sacred, the emotional, and the timeless. The poet's words are truly a tribute to love, resilience, and the beauty of the human spirit, making this book a valuable addition to the world of contemporary poetry. May each reader find solace, inspiration, and understanding within these pages.

Krishna Bless!

SUBHA R   **1-11-2024**
BBA - JDM (Manipal Institute of Jewellery Management),
Manipal University – 1st Rank Holder & Gold Medalist
MBA, (Marketing), School of Management, Manipal University

FOREWORD

"Premanjali" – selected love poems written by Dr. C.V. Ravindranath conveys the power of love, spirituality, devotion and nature and it's interconnectedness of all beings. It celebrates the Universality of love - A love free from bondage and not constrained by religious doctrines and dogmas. In these poems, Beauty of Mother Nature is beautifully mirrored in the essence of a womanhood. Both embody grace, strength and nurturing qualities.

The poems like 'Red Sun', 'Fantasy and Reality', 'Kadalamma', 'Feelings', 'Universal Love', 'Monsoon affairs', 'and Small yet Sweet' intertwines the elements of Nature with the experience of love, suggesting that both are powerful and transformative forces. The connection between nature and the beauty of a woman is beautifully reflected in poems that emphasize nurturing, passion, and love. The poet expresses his devotion and profound love for Shiva, Shakti, Ganesh, Jesus Christ, Buddha, and Krishna consciousness through his poems. He also conveys his respect and admiration to the Mystics such as Osho, Avadhoot Baba Shivananda ji and Chinmayananda ji.

His poems, like the spirited festivals of Kerala and feeding bottles, reflect his resentment toward alcoholism, transforming God's Own Country into a hell.

Poems like Aloneness, Death- a Great Celebration! expresses the element of detachment in one's spiritual journey.

"Tears of the Veil" and **"Wife's Deed"** depict the dominance of male chauvinism in society and the sacrifices women make as they struggle to support their families to make ends meet.

The poet expresses his distress and anguish towards current issues of the world like Terrorism, Natural disasters like Tsunami, Religio-Political Ideologies and Fundamentalism.

Dear reader, I hope these poems touch your heart as profoundly as they touched ours.

ॐ**Adi Paraashaktiye Namah:**

SANITA R   **01.11.24**
BHM, MBA (USA)

RED SUN

Unto her love the hot Sun succumbs,
Kissing the trembling lips of the waves,
The Ocean of love seductively dances,
To the highest peak of overwhelming ecstasy,
Enlightening Him to golden "RED – SUN".

30th May 1996

ALONENESS

You can be alone always,
But lonely never once,
In His company so graceful,
Meditating on your grief,
Being a light unto thyself,
Never losing smiles,
In life so beautiful!

2nd January 2006

FANTASY AND REALITY

Full moon shy away at her brightness,
Glow of her spotless milky fairness,
Gleaming looks of youthful indulgence,
Imposing lips of hidden naughtiness,
Inviting my love of aesthetic careness!

Sparkling nose stud lose its brilliance,
While her smile outshine all starry brightness,
Well set pearls of glowing freshness,
Like a full moon glorifying all darkness,
Fluttering locks her tufty softness!

Rosy buds twinkle like a honeydew,
Blooming flowers of springtime hue,
Butterflies and honeybees slue,
Sucking their divine nectar of joy,
Fondling them all her passions grew!

Her slender hip cannot bear the onslaught,
The thundering strokes of lightning heat,
Of thumping beats of palpitating heart,
Swinging body surge beads of sweat,
Falling into my hands of caressing treat!

Nature's splendid hidden cave of treasures,
Open up the mystical doors of heavenly pleasures,
When my magical wand of love sparkles,
Tracing her soothing strains of passionate lores,
Getting lost to this world of aesthetic reality!

3rd September 2006

TEARS OF THE VEIL

Sati out of insults plunged herself into the fire,
Sita to prove purity compelled to stride over the fire,
Domination of male chauvinism not too rare,
In the religious dogmas of holy wear,
Which every Motherhood painfully bear,
To cradle humanity with utmost care.

Chopping off her breasts once he warmly cuddled,
For his own sensual pleasures he muddled,
In the journey of mankind he saddled,
The objects of sexual provocation rattled,
Under the veil her natural instinct curtailed,
Veiling her feminine feelings got bridled.

Once worshipped as the Goddess of Nature,
Kundalini Shakthi of great sons rupture,
Enlightening this soul with divine culture,
Teaching the world a promise of the future,
Binding humanity with love to endure,
Compassion which man had suckled to ensure.

Fundamentalism slave her as condemned,
Manusmrithi, Torah, Hadith and Talmud,
Curse her beauty which divinity hath bestowed,
To travail souls from womb to tomb, so sacred,
Universal journey of consciousness transcend,
Glorifying humanity to be ultimately evolved.

8th November 2006

PREMANJALI

DEATH – A GREAT CELEBRATION!

Death is like the day and the night,

The wink of the sun, the lord of the light,

Yet death is of great fright,

Who fails to know its might,

To transcend soul to higher flight!

Like birth, we have no choice,

So silent .... it has no voice,

'ween two, love is the only grace,

Making our karmas for better cause,

Taking our souls to higher phase!

Father and Mother, we can't select,

Not even a blood relation we can elect,

A mysterious family of divine sect,

Yet humanity fights for unknown set,

Of doctrines and dogmas of religious vent!

Whether rich or poor we all go,

From womb to tomb a travel to forego,

The past karmas carried upon ego,

Until we empty all our tempo,

Of suppression and repression of self manifesto!

Little by little we always die daily,

Living our destiny we wrote minutely,

Learning the art of dying so deliberately,

Unknowingly knowing the unknown solely,

On the divine path of the soul eternally!

Live a life with profound determination,

Bring forth the latent talents unto manifestation,

to add the share of our divine contribution,

In the universal drama of human evolution,

Making our death a great celebration!

23rd November 2006

SHIVA - SHAKTHI

Shivam is energy static,
While Shakthi a kinetic,
Making universe energetic,
Where nature appears dualistic!

Merging of he and she in unity,
Creating a universal family,
A habitat of opposite polarity,
To attain unity among diversity!!

Yin and Yang being life-force divinity,
Keeping mass and energy in sanity,
Propelling ecstasy and creativity,
Where life is but a journey to eternity!!!

3rd October 2008

WIFE'S DEED

Mother is always an outcome of a wife,
Being a bride is to begin again a life,
Until she gives birth to a legitimate babe,
Life cycle is never biologically complete!

Then how can you decry a wife,
Pitching against the mother's care,
Did she not sacrifice her whole life,
In making you a father so wise!

Without pinching his delicate ego,
She caressed his starved limbo,
Awakening creativity out of erotic porno,
Enslaving herself, all her joy to forego!

Caring your kids to grow with love,
To take your name in a world of pride,
Nothing in gratitude did she crave,
Selfless service indeed wives serve!

Mothers are lucky to get him so tender,
Wives pity to care him when so older,
By virtue mothers are simply rare,
To rock the cradle of life to pair!

Mother loves her own blood and flesh,
But wife has to love a stranger afresh,
Harmonizing a society without a clash,
Promoting a family of his paternal wish!

Yet mothers take all the credit,
Leaving wives' services all in doubt,
A thankless job of abused debt,
Oh man, can you repay her holy deed!

Only a good wife whose affection,
Make a good mother of compassion,
Loving all children with same passion,
But possessiveness create confusion!

Nectar of both tastes verily the same,
Only cord of relationships separate,
This bondage of life scripted by nature,
Where conflicts resolve out of your care!

Oh man, why not respect her as a Mother?

4th October 2008

PARVATHI

Mother nature is Goddess Shakthi,
Without her energy there is no canopy,
To shelter all manifestations under her mercy,
Where mass and energy move in symphony,
Revolution of heavenly bodies in synchrony!

In her secured womb seeds groom,
Out of her sacred love-play flowers bloom,
To fulfill their everlasting urge to blossom,
Their dreams of love in vivid colours to loom,
A universal family with love in their bosom!

Father of universe is her Lord Shivam,
The static state of silence in vacuum,
Out of which derive her kinetic momentum,
To bless the universe to keep a spiritual decorum,
Showering divine compassion upon Humanism!

5th October 2008

SHIVA

A spellbound silence of nothingness,
Dark bluish vacuum of divine peacefulness,
A sanctum sanctorum of powerful absoluteness,
Shiva the father of universal consciousness,
Wedded to the mother nature of playfulness!

In the universal drama of Parvathi's presentation,
He is the spark of divinity in her manifestation,
Where each soul has its own destination,
A flight of ecstasy in this silent meditation,
Desirelessness being its solid foundation!!

A journey to the highest realms of consciousness,
Where truth leads to choiceless awareness,
A timeless space of splendid godliness,
An eternal compassion of blissfulness,
Feelings of Shivoham in the inner emptiness!!!

5th October 2008

KADALAMMA
(MOTHER OCEAN)

With raging spirit she dances in seduction,
Spreading her laced gown drenched in temptation,
Little did I wonder the reason for her celebration,
Cajoling and winning her lover in bloody molestation,
The red sun succumbs to her dusky embracement!

Out of this love affair, all creatures descend,
With his holy rays, evolution ascend,
Onto her silky waves, civilizations blend,
The cultural entity of a universal mould,
Spreading the philosophy of brotherhood!

Her colours change to the tunes of his moods,
Romantically blue in the summer rains,
Torrentially hue when the monsoon beats,
Thunderously rude while the hurricane hits,
Devastating the world of negative vibes,
When man pollutes for the greedy needs!

Again the ocean dances in resurrection,
Cleansing all our sins in redemption!

8th October 2008

GANESHA

Remover of all obstacles is Vigneshwara,
All Gods seek His boons even Parvati-n-Shiva,
Elephant headed and pot bellied Buddha,
Of Indian mythology and ancient Vedanta,
The copywriter of holy Mahabharatha,
Expressed orally by the great sage Vyasa!

Residing in us at Muladhara Chakra,
Deity of Kundalini to erupt to Supra,
A surge unto universal intelligentsia,
A spring of compassionate euphoria,
Dancing to the beats of Vinayaka:
Ganapathi bapa moriya! Mangala murthi moriya!!

14th October 2008

TERRORISTS

All Muslims aren't terrorists,
But now, all terrorists are Muslims,
The children of fundamentalism,
Hard core Islamic extremism,
Which horrified the whole world,
By the sword of the holy Jihad:
The gates of heaven open on death,
To martyrs of Islam for their heroic worth!

Born out of poverty and deprivations,
Uncared children of desperations,
Fathered by polygamous aggressions,
Borne by mothers of suppressions,
Unemployed youths of demographic explosions,
Misled by extreme religious conditionings,
Ishmael's creed of warring Bedouin nomadic tribes,
Born out of Sarah – Abraham – Hagar couples!

Jihad is the war of their vengeance,
Born out of Sarah- n- Hagar family conflicts,
Where Isaac- n- Ishmael claimed their rights,
Over Jerusalem as their ancestral place,
Engaging their creeds to wage holy wars,
Judaism – Christianity – Islam being their casualties,
Of their unsettled ancient disputes,
Which terrorise the world out of peace!

Religiosity of Israel thus spake,
Words of Torah, Bible and Koran speak,
 A story of the same kinds of Adam-n Eve,
Settling their chores for silly vibes,
Bringing chaos to a world so meek,
Killing their own kins for stupid vie,
A lesson to be learned, why families break,
When religions fail to hold them as folks!

Amidst animalistic traits and chaos,
A warrior was born to set moral rules,
For this wandering tribe of the Arabic sands,
The poem of Koran thus sung to his ears,
Revealed by Allah -o- Akbar to the last one,
He married eight to save their plights,
Allowed others to marry four as their rights,
Hadith and Sharia being their sacred laws!

Mohammed Nabi, thus became the last prophet,
To save Arabia out of the worst hit,
Turmoil of burning religious conflict,
By his sword of peace, Islam's final verdict,
To usher in ethics and morality at its best,
Misled by his sword their children fight,
To establish a world of Islamic fundamental right,
Fought by terrorist outfits aggressive might!

Secularism and non-violence beyond their reach,
Law of shariat clouded their divine search,
Conditioned mind of prophetic madrassa preach,
Holy wars against Kafir unlatch,
Terrorising the world by their distinct catch,
Proxy war waged by their bloody twitch,
Drinking for their political thirst to quench,
Murdering innocent children of the same hatch!

Terrorism is not in the weapons they teach,
But in the fallen minds of the evil ditch,
Enlightenment through morphogenic pitch,
Meditation being the bioplasmic stitch,
To repair the torn mind from nuclear splash,
Saving this beautiful earth of Allah's wish,
To uphold the moral ethics in order to wash,
The stains of blood-n-tears of human anguish!

25th December 2008 X-mas day wish

JESUS CHRIST

An incarnation of love and compassion,
Son of Vishwakarma by profession,
Jesus taught the world to enlighten,
By redeeming other's suffering pain,
Sacrificing one's life for the holy divine!

A symbol of non-violence, simple-n-sweet,
Leading in love the world to unite,
In the name of the Father-n- the holy spirit,
Universalism being its core sprite,
Crucifixion made Him a Christ!

Never He built a church to preach,
Never He wrote a Bible to teach,
Yet made the world to enrich,
With love, the existential search,
Resurrecting mankind to be unselfish!

25th December 2008

GAUTHAM: THE WAY OF BUDDHA

Buddha is the master of all masters,
Who made a quantum leap to other shores,
The only man in the human history of wises,
Who scaled the highest peak of consciousness,
Yet delved into the deepest core of human minds,
Contradicting all organized religions,
Which lead humanity to utter chaos,
Dhammapada being his basic teachings,
Nirvana being mankind's ultimate growth,
Nothingness being the only existential Truth !

9th February 2009

MY SILENT PRAYER

O Mother Parashakthi,
Beauty of Cosmic energy,
Manifestation of Shiva Shakthi,
Transcend upon me!
Transform me!!
Transfigure me!!!

Remove all my desires,
Past memories and thoughts,
Until my mind drops,
Unto your divine silence,
Invoking Universal Intelligence,
Compassion, harmony and peace,
Thus self-knowledge perceives,
The ultimate realms of truth and bliss!

6th April 2009

POLITICIAN

A politician requires three big essentials:
A thick skin which never tears,
A big mouth which never tires,
An ugly wife who never attracts!

His tongue is too long enough,
To tickle the dead ideals so tough,
Corrupting the mass mind to rough,
Conflicts of disputing religious stuff!

The destructive mass mind of mad,
Parasiting the public fund earned hard,
With politricks so awkward,
The last resort of a coward!

Citizens of the world let us unite,
We have nothing to lose yet,
But only stupid politicians of fright,
To make this earth a lovely retreat!

30th April 2009

PREMANJALI

EYES OF INTELLIGENCE

Her eyes shine so sparkling bright,
Like a full moon on a dark lake light,
Where lotus bloom on a silvery float,
Twinkling stars ponder deep into my heart,
Tingling my senses of passion to melting hot!

Sensitive to Her vibes my senses lose,
Where the power of ego always resists,
Vanishing of me welcomes the grace,
Of compassion and love make me dance,
Celebrating life in magnanimous ways!

Life is but only relationships weary,
Dependence of several beings worry,
The world full of silly drama of merry,
Where we enact again our roles of ecstasy,
Trusting one another in this mysterious journey!

Eyes of intelligence open our way to wisdom,
Transcending to the truth of Her and Him,
Breaking the bondage of all stupid religionism,
Invoking universal intelligentsia of spiritualism,
Where our souls dance to the tunes of naturalism!

Can we quench our thirst and dream,
In such a game of competing team,
Forgoing the basic instinct of materialism,
Drenching ourselves unto true humanism,
Amidst dreadful waves of oceanic mysticism!

3rd June 2009

HARTAL

A political weapon of violence,
Sheathed in the blood of vengeance,
To terrorize the people of innocence,
A mask to hide their ignorance,
Politicians throw their arrogance!

A socio – political hindrance,
To push our state to backwardness,
Hampering our kids' transcendence,
To higher state of consciousness,
Curbing their rights of awareness!

Killing the productivity of all business,
Devastation of bloody utterances,
Destroying social harmony and peace,
Democratic chaos of governance,
Parasiting the public investments!

Hartal a great curse of disturbance,
Against a society of intelligence,
Converting into an alcoholic inheritance,
Losing ethos of cultural and moral conscience,
A mass persecution of human perseverance!

20th June 2009

BIRTHDAY GIFT

From the Mother's womb we're born only once,
Celebrating the birthday in life only once,
All other days are celebrated as death days,
'Cause we die here now at all moments,
To our attachments, jealousy, hatred, fears-n-sorrows!

In birth, we have no much choices,
Neither our parents nor any relationships,
Not even a family of our choicest longings,
'Cause the wheel of life spins by his karmas,
Of what he deserves than he desires!

In life, the only choice is friendship,
Love being its only companionship,
Where compassion being the idol of worship,
With mutual respect and trusteeship,
A gift of love, full of birthday fellowship!

Cheers and bottoms – up!!!

24th August 2009

FEELINGS

My feelings unto thee is compassion,
The never ending waves of the ocean,
Depth of trust is the treasure hidden,
Where the wind breeze the sorrows ridden,
When the red sun kisses thy blue horizon!

Thousand eyes watch the celebration,
The galaxy of divine constellation,
Where we hold each other in consolation,
In life's tragedy of separation,
Yet our souls meet in unification!

24th August 2009

BEYOND THE DARK CLOUDS!

A chubby tot treads chasing the waves,
Under the canopy of the sun ever shines,
Inspiring her feats of bubbling joy smiles,
On the golden sands lay etched her footprints,
The landmark of her life here now begins!

Giggling screams spread her naughty youth,
Jumping over the waves prove her sweet worth,
Stunning the worldly men of great strength,
Inviting their attention for romantic growth,
Glorifying the motherly touch on this earth!!

Soon dusk falls blinding the red sun,
Life dying to the great thrill with no gain,
The old lady tracing her prints in pain,
Searching for a glimpse with great strain,
Beyond the dark clouds hidden in vain!!!

30th August 2009

PREMANJALI

THE SPIRITED FESTIVALS OF KERALA

Lost to their culture, Malayalees always,
Celebrate their holy festivals with drinks,
Replacing the traditional feast on banana leaves,
With chicken biriyani and highly spirited bottles,
Boozing has become their spirited holy rituals,
Whether it be Vishu, Onam, Ramzan or X-mas,
Birth, marriage and death the main ceremonies,
From womb to tomb, a kick of joyous agonies!

No wonder Vivekananda called her a mad house,
Though Mahabali ruled her enviously casteless,
God's own country in his time being classless,
Bountifully splendid by nature's blessings,
Yet socio-politically-n-culturally bottled in spirits:
Now the devil's workshop of intoxicating holiness,
Procreating children of alcoholic inheritance,
Miscreants of all abuses and chaos,
Alas, we're ashamed to be her descendants!

3rd September 2009

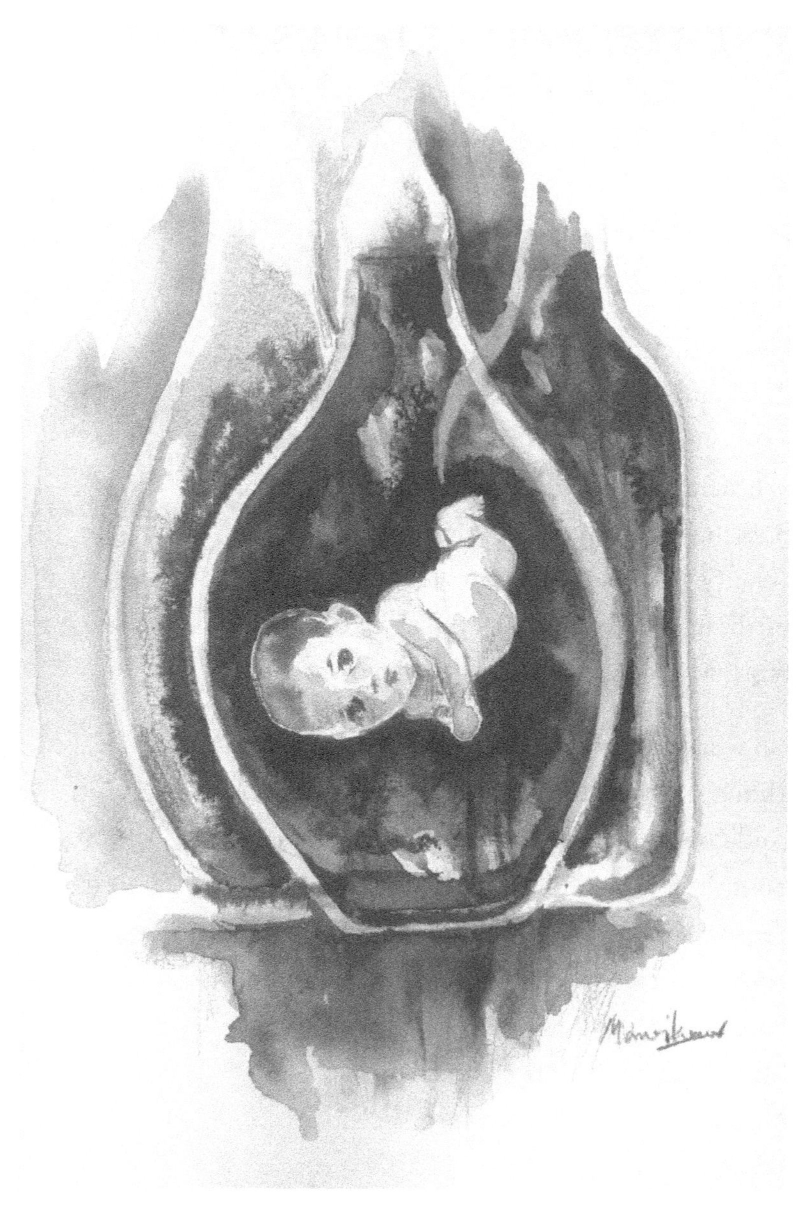

PREMANJALI

FEEDING BOTTLES!

Moms denied their milky breasts,
To maintain their vital statistics:
Thirty-six, twenty-four, thirty-six!

Babies are forced to feeding bottles,
Losing moms' warmth and caress,
Kids got habituated to cola bottles!

Compassion got lost in youths,
Due to their passion to bottles,
Tingling their kicks to cocktails!

Intoxicating venom into their nerves,
Floating a generation of drunkards,
A stupid world of pissed vagabonds,
Abusing social ethos and ethics!

Unless moms feed their breasts,
Men are bound to fall for bottles!

4th September 2009

Dedicated to my favourite Tamil Poet, Thiru Kannadasan.

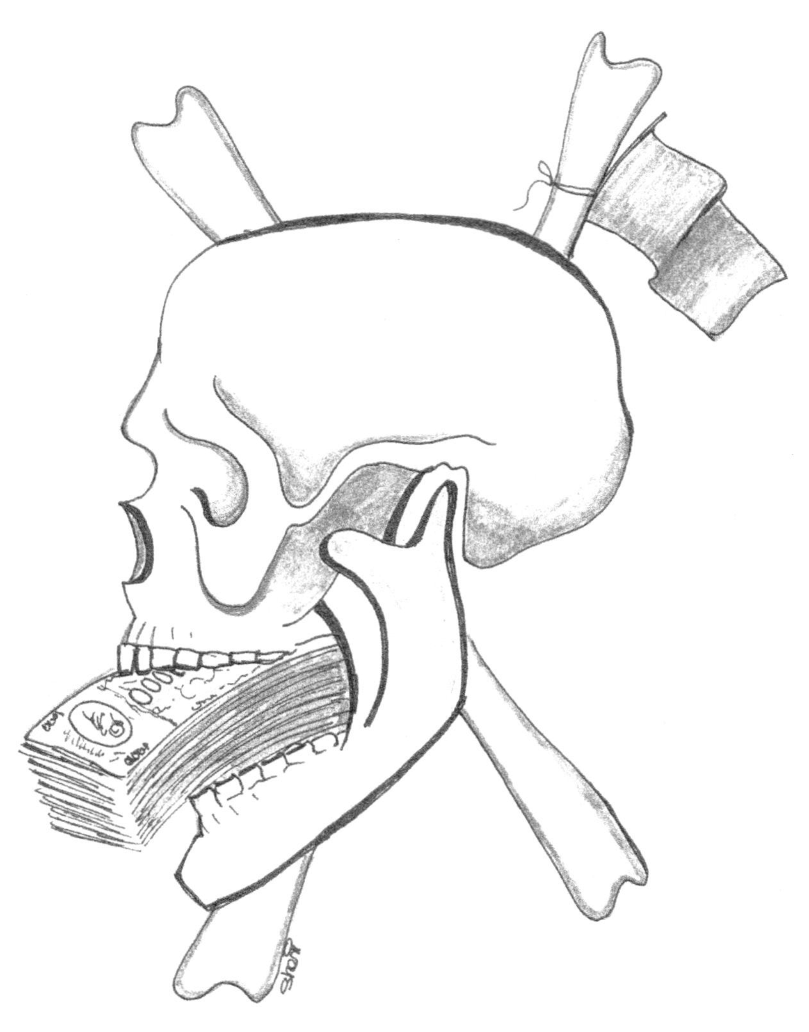

PREMANJALI

VISION, MISSION AND COMMISSION!

Thirsty to become rich, famous and pop,

Over the morality and ethics we gallop,

By overnight to saddle on the top,

Where even eagles dare to soar up,

Lest lost to the dark clouds of flip!

Lost to the insight of great vision,

Man plunders the world with commission,

From womb to tomb the only mission,

To gather fast buck we all envision,

Creating a life full of high tension!

Money thus earned wasted on medicine,

For the survival of our own children,

Born out of our shady business win,

To cleanse the deeds of our own sin,

We hammer the last nail in their coffin!

Yet mankind hasn't learned any lesson!!

In vain of that devastating quotation!!!

24th September 2009

KRISHNA CONSCIOUSNESS

Nishkama karma being the very basics,
Of Krishna's universal Vedanta teachings,
Where we crave no fruits for our deeds,
Thus doing action for the sake of action less,
Without gathering karmic imprints in race,
Proclaiming karma yoga the highest grace!

Out of karma yoga universal love is born,
A compassion, unconditional to everyone,
An energy to hold together each one,
A fundamental universal phenomenon,
For manifestation of life in meditation,
Of he and she in divine blissful union!

Out of compassion bhakthi is hence formed,
Where total devotion showers the Beloved,
When Radha merges with Krishna in sacred,
Ecstasy being the divine music wedded,
With no separation altogether with God,
Spreading positive vibration to the world!

Out of devotion, awareness of wisdom invoked,
Knowledge not of the past conditioned mind,
Never of the memories holy scriptures doctrine,
Nor expounded by any great guru however blessed,
A benediction of the cosmic energy thus nurtured,
A life search for Truth in this pathless land urged!

30th September 2009

AVADHOOT BABA SHIVANANDA

Avadhoot Baba Shivananda,
Blessed by Sadguru Nithyananda,
To be a sage of Siddha – Loka,
To bless the devotees in Shiva-yoga!

Attired in blazing blood-red, he strides,
Glorifying the Shiva-Shakti, he signifies,
The power of kundalini so glorifies,
The energy of seven-chakra magnifies!

Big piercing eyes showering empathy,
Loud grave voice rendering sympathy,
Huge solid hands blessing prosperity,
Whole environment blasted with energy!

The sleeping serpent got aroused verily,
Trembling the spinal cord surprisingly,
The inner joy surpassed our boundary,
To the highest joy of spiritual ecstasy!

Is he a Tantrik with mystical powers,
Or a Zen master with a belly full of laughter,
Nay, he could be a Buddha, full of silence,
Showering benediction upon all meditators!

Join me my friends to be under his grace,
Specially chosen by him to raise,
Our Kundalini powers to aesthetic praise,
The journey of our life to spiritualize!

When the disciple is ready,
The Master has arrived already,
Bestowing his ever-lasting energy,
Upon our eternal divine body!

26th August 2004

BEAUTY AND THE BRUTE

To be a beauty is a gift of God,
For all the virtues being divinely blessed,
Beauty, brain and boon very rarely blend,
For these qualities together never to find,
Yet a sweet maiden fit to be crowned,
Lived in his heart, soon to be drowned!

Such a beauty walked into the wild range,
Where the brute ruled with a revenge,
The king of the beasts never failed to avenge,
Without bothering to possess anything to savage,
Unmoved by his wildness the beauty rose to rage,
To tame these animalistic traits to siege!

Thunderous laughs never shattered her peace,
Scandalizing looks never changed her poise,
Seductive moves never stopped her motives,
Lustful speeches never bothered her ears,
The king of wild got perplexed by her vibes,
Fascinated by her bewitching looks!

Sparkling looks pierce his heart to bear,

Lovely hands soothe his body to care,

Whispering voice lifts his spirit to soar,

Innocent smile washes away his deep sore,

Caressing being sure to be her true nature,

The crowned empress of his inner shrine!

She knew the chemistry of alchemy bold,

To transform the base metals into pure gold,

Surprising smooch from her sensuous lips told,

That smothery only can capture the hard,

Like the ocean softens the rock so solid,

Shaping the uncut diamond to a sparkling brand!

Stunt by her soothing advances never surpass,

Poor brute could never resist to suppress,

The basic instinct provoked by the Goddess,

By overwhelming love he lifted her to possess,

And made a quantum leap to embarrass,

The gushing waterfall onto a lonely island of virgin bliss!

11th April 2005

BEAUTY – MY DARLING!

Lean and slender she walked into our life,
To leave a mark of love in her grave,
Under the golden red canopy survive,
A nature-loving family of five,
Watching her feats on the sands, so alive!

Black and tall, darling of our home,
Dedicated to serve her best, she roams,
To save us all from the venom,
Which the serpent spurt in the farm,
In the courtyard, making our 'Red-Sun' gloom!

Lost the precious prize we have ever won,
In the race of friendship which man has ever run,
A faithful friend which our memory has ever seen,
Oh lord, take care of her in your shrine,
Never send her back again for such a ruin!

Black is beautiful, beauty my dear,
Ever dear you shall remain near,
Carved in golden letters so clear,
Your name in our family memoir,
Sleep in peace, man's best friend forever!

29th March 2001

JOURNEY OF A SAIL-LESS BOAT

Life is like a sail-less boat,
Jumping up and down to the waves beat,
Taking others to ride in your empty space,
Shattering all your dreams and peace!

For some used your brains to mint,
Others stroll over your body to drain,
Each one of them having all fun and gain,
Shattering all your dreams insane!

For the gain of some, name and fame,
You have been cheated by the same,
Among all those sensuous toy game,
Shattering all your dreams by a dame!

Never trust a dame in wine,
She shall offer anything to dine,
Awaken to see you are in vain,
Shattering all your dreams by a sin!

She shall give the body but not soul,
To reap high riches of her hell,
Showering lust for molesting your braille,
Shattering all your dreams until you fail!

5th March 2002

THE CURSE OF LOVE

Fly back to me sweetheart,
On a winglet of a sweet dream,
To bring back those tunes of your love songs,
Which I had torn in my youthful days,
For which my heart is smashed,
By the waves of the Ocean of love, so crude!

Like a monsoon's rage, the sea is rough,
Ruining the journey of my life so tough,
Until I pay my repentance to thee,
She shall never be calm and serene,
Eroding all the rocks where I hide,
Rejecting thy love so pure and sincere!

Life shall never pardon me, dear,
Until you forgive this sinner,
Who had once rejected your heart's cry,
For which each wave splash to try,
Breaking my heart into pieces they lie,
On the dry sands of life's journey!

Gathering my kids from her torment wind,
Breaking all my world by her torrent wave,
Leave me alone at least for their plight,
A request from a father's beaten fight,
Who had once rejected your love so divine,
To its tune he had forgotten to rejoice!

I shall then come back to you as a saint,
Standing before you, conscious pure and faint,
All the winds and waves shall then stop to hear,
His heart's own poetry whispering into your ear,
Immortal shall be thy love, never to die,
Disappearing into the misty mountains never to lie!

18th March 2002

DREAMS COME TRUE!

Dreams are like butterflies,
Fluttering on their sexy wings,
Soaring high into the blue skies,
Making our destination to success,
Fulfilling all our dreams come true!

Psychedelic wings fluttering gracefully,
Propelling ambition and determination simultaneously,
Knowledge being the body energising eventually,
All the three encouraging our willpower synchronizingly,
Fulfilling all our dreams come true!

Without knowledge we shall miss the stars,
Gaining them our life's biggest tasks,
Even knowing we could mislead the texts,
Intuition being its secret of secrets,
Fulfilling all our dreams come true!

Success only comes to those of Positivity,
And failure soon to those of Negativity,
Meditation being the key to Creativity,
Elevating our consciousness intuitively,
Fulfilling all our dreams come true!

Success comes like a benediction,
To ego-less efforts put in with compassion,
Unto His service, we lay in salvation,
The whole existence pouring back in affection,
Until we dream this in solicitation,
How can our dreams come true?

17th January 2004

GOLDEN BLONDE

Deep beneath my heart,
Had a crave for blonde,
Maybe the shine of gold,
Which sparkled this thought!

Peaceful eyes so green,
Like an oasis on a sandy dune,
Beads of pearls clearly seen,
Like pebbles in an ocean so clean!

Like a moon her face glisten,
Smiling under the veil of golden brown,
The golden locks of love brighten,
Unto the tunes of my thought so divine!

Her looks are soothing glee,
Her eyelashes flutter in flee,
When her tiny rosy lips split into two,
Unto the strains of my heart so true!

Filled with compassion her budding blossom bloom,
When the sun teases her teenage dream,
Caught unaware of her joyous scream,
Unto his warmth the buds transform!

Chiseled out of a soft marble,

Her splendid body-shape marvel,

Like a valley flow so natural,

Seducing all my senses to sparkle!

Locks of gold, which he can never forget,

Bond of love, which she can never meet,

Saddened to his heart she departs,

The star beyond my horizon never set!

Golden Blonde on the golden sands,

When the golden red sun shines,

Singing and swinging to the tunes,

Of his hearty poems written on the waves!!!

10th December 2003

KILLER TSUNAMI!!!

Out of the rubble many hands protrude still,
Maybe their last call against Nature's will,
What wrong had they committed they know not still,
For the killer Tsunami has washed away all their thrill,
Upon this devastating tragedy we all yell!

Not a priest or a pundit was able to smell,
The catastrophe which had stricken one and all,
Turning deaf to their prayers mankind trail,
For all their atrocities to create this hell,
Yet, mankind gathers knowledge again to fail!

Worms, birds and animals smell this danger awful,
For they are the blessed ones here to prevail,
One with Nature always joyously playful,
Without man's ego piercingly so cruel,
Yet, mankind learn lessons only to fail!

Culprits are those learned standing so tall,
With their high intelligentsia mere fragile,
Only to fight religiously so powerful,
Hurting Mother Earth, being so unnatural,
Unto dust their wisdom still crumble!

Where are your powerful politicians gone?
Where are your brainy scientists gone?
Where are your religious leaders gone?
Hiding themselves in comfort they go on,
Preaching those vengeful doctrines insane!

Yet, mankind hasn't learned any lesson at all!!!

8th January 2005

LEGACY OF A DANCER

Irresistible eyes sparkle expressions,
Moist eyelashes sprinkle compassions,
Black eyeballs grace sentiments,
Slim eyebrows keep the rhythm of feelings,
Unto her pulsation throb our little hearts!

Each mudra mean a sign of divinity,
Her whole body palpitates with joy,
Electrifying the crowd, our mind and body,
When the blushing sun painted red our canopy,
Over the open beach garden on the Arabian sea!

Dancing waves fail to keep her steps,
Danseuse disappearing unto her dance,
Dumb found, the winds mend their ways,
Pregnant clouds resist their summer dews,
For a spectacular concert, her feet renders!

Trees and flowers shower their blessings,
Swaying hither and thither to her movements,
Even the moon kept lurking her sensuous steps,
Provoking my soul to join her dance so joyously,
Captivating me in her rendezvous of blissful ecstasy!

30th April 2002

LUST

When the divine love is lost in thy heart,
The devilish lust clouds thy sight,
Every lustful look sends a sexual vibe,
Blinding thy eyes to be an immoral slave!

When the urge is shot, then the heart is shut,
Sensuous lips sprout open to molest,
The mind is feverish and head is burdened,
For the gushing blood to be descended!

Breath has lost its sensible beat,
Depth of thy genetics crave to treat,
Unto this madden moments youth is lost,
Only to weep over the broken heart frustrate!

Animalistic imprints imbibe your traits again and again,
Until you are deprived of love, never to be forsaken,
Never to reach in life that state of enlighten,
Entertaining oneself in each other's fun and sin!

Out of this relationship so shady,
You give birth to the world so badly,
Feeding thy breasts of lust and sexy,
Creating them to crave for money and body!

Those who are lost to the lust,
Shall never win a beloved until last,
Alas, if you miss the love to meet,
Your soul shall never meet the ultimate!

In the search of love, you behold the beloved,
Until the ego melts to open thy heart,
Then the divinity shall sparkle to be graced,
Thy soul shall forever be blessed!

"BE BLESSED BY THE DIVINE."

5th March 2002

MONSOON AFFAIRS

Lo! it takes exactly nine months passionately,
For the clouds to get pregnant again merrily,
The romance between the Sun and Earth cosmically,
Even human kind imitate them so naturally!

Waves swing high to clasp the heavenly clouds,
To hug, kiss and suckle their tender blooms,
Drinking their nectar, the ocean quench her thirst,
What a sacred affair they have it in rains!

Impregnated clouds burst into blessings,
Showering upon this Earth for her beings,
For blossoming, blooming and celebrations,
Nature's divine affair to sustain evolutions!

Seeds sprout out to become youthful shoots,
Plants crave to mature old as trees,
Blossoming unto flowers and fruits, spreading seeds,
Fulfilling unconditional love affair of all living beings!

Yet, why man shy away from all festivities,
Fearing thunderous cloudy monsoon rains,
Avoiding even those wet honeymoon and romances,
When nature beckons such a romantic ambience!

Let's cuddle in Her umbrella with our beloveds,
Whispering hearty love songs unto our sweethearts,
Teasing those waves on the wettish golden sands,
Behind the cloudy veil the red sun kisses her sensuous lips!

Man should learn more of Nature's divine lessons,
Bringing fulfillment in their life of actions,
Where nature plays her own universal laws,
Lo! Microcosms verily transcend macrocosms!

22nd June 2005

SHIVOHAM! SHIVOHAM!! SHIVOHAM!!!

Shivoham is a state of oneness with the universe,

Where you shall lose all your mind's conditionings,

Until you merge with the nothingness,

Disappearing unto the cosmic energy of divine Godliness!

Shivoham is your empty inner space,

Stillness of your genetic centre,

Where all beings meet at the universal centre,

A static point around all particles move!

Shivoham is the absolute truth,

Beyond time, space and breath,

Beyond life, birth and death,

Superconscious state at the ultimate!

Shivoham! Shivoham!! Shivoham!!!

18th March 2002

SMALL YET SWEET

Small yet sweet is the most beautiful,
Like butterflies and bees flutter so graceful,
Soft and fluffy they are very wonderful,
Like babies and birds so playful.

Innocent eyes are very watchful,
Cherry lips smack so merciful,
Blooming buds bubble so lovable,
My heart breaks unto her pleasurable!

Unto her love's threshold so painful,
Her joyous trace beyond bountiful,
Gathering her gasp too excitable,
Merging of souls so fanciful!

17th April 2003

SPIRITUALITY

Spirituality has nothing to do with religions,
Nothing to do with Krishna, Buddha or Christ,
Nothing to do with Temple, Mosque or Church,
Nothing to do with rituals, ideals or Gods,
It is your inner growth, inner journey to the unknown!

Journey of aloneness, not loneliness,
One goal for all, but path being different,
Objectless desire of your inner core,
When your dormant energy strives to awaken,
Creativity blossoms as the first step to spirituality!

Same energy exploded in your sexual urge,
Extension of your being, totally excreted at your death,
When creativity rises sexuality decreases,
Thus it is nearer to spirituality,
Lo, sexuality transcends to spirituality!

Its transcendence is called yoga,
And its process is meditation,
Its benediction is creativity,
Its ultimate state is ecstasy,
Guru being only a light for your dark path!

When the disciple is ready,
The Guru shall appear steady,
Faith and purity the only eligibility,
Let us surrender at His lotus feet,
For a beautiful journey called Spirituality!

19th March 2002

THE LAST RITES

Drenched in early waters, wet hands clapped thrice,
An invitation to our ancestors presided by dark crows,
To partake the rice in congregation to remove all sins,
The last rites to the beloved who eternally sleeps,
A homage paid to lay the soul in peaceful bliss!

No crows visited on my call so religious,
Making the Brahmin so stupid and furious,
Questioning my sincerity they all criticize,
Ashamed I gazed the golden sun to confess,
My innocence over this undine ghostly meal!

Out of blue flashed some crazy ideas,
Of mixing the chicken curry with the rice,
Suddenly crows in tens gathered to our surprise,
Crowing and pecking uninvited even for once,
Perhaps mocking our stupidity at orthodox beliefs!

Even the crows have changed in times,
Their scavenging habits for better taste buds,
Now they dine only on rich non-veg meals,
Wasted in abundance after sumptuous feasts,
Alas, mankind always remain in superstitiousness!!!

16th March 2005

THE LIGHT OF DARKNESS

Light, a symbol of faith from time, immemorial,
Whether be Hinduism, Christianity or Islamic call,
Thousand suns rise together in your religious trail,
Eternal light being the trademark so spiritual,
Adorned in the sanctum sanctorum of every temple,
Invoking the highest benediction of divine spell!

Light zooms faster to the farthest star,
Illuminating our Mother Earth so far,
A tribute paid to the superstar,
Who gallops in a chariot of seven horses fair,
The source of energy for all living beings to share,
Redeemer of darkness in our lives to care!

Though light so great runs so fast,
Only second to darkness which exists first,
Before light could arrive darkness already persist,
Out of darkness everything born to exist,
Nothingness is its true nature dealt,
Whether it be a big–bang theory read,
Or a black–hole principle strongly held!

We all are born out of pitch darkness,
Yet we all fear of its scary wilderness,
Light may represent the learned sacredness,
Yet mankind kills all beings in its empty darkness,
Negative, evil and bad thoughts of preference,
Their same illogical utterances of sad religiousness!

Light may grace the plants and animals,
But no sun ever shines in all human minds,
Because they are conditioned in doctrines,
On the call of a politician or a priest's utterance,
Breaking the hearts they inflict vengeance,
Still humanity procreates in utter darkness!

Light has never reached all destinations,
Of peace, love, freedom and happiness,
Where politics, religion and business,
Lead the whole humanity in violence,
Only death shall know its greatness,
When the soul soars high unto emptiness!

Thus whispered Shiva into the ears of His consort,
The beauty of the darkest of the dark night,
To merge with His energy when we meditate,
Thus spake Buddha again of this state,
Of Vipasana, a method so highly great,
Leading humanity unto enlightenment!

Never can light conquer darkness,
Like life over death in race,
For it persists always in this Universe,
Yonder where sun fails to rise,
Thus light is limited to grace,
When our little palms cover our face!

So what divinity light has so great to praise,
Even if it removes all darkness of this Universe,
Unless it shines in human hearts to rise!!!

11th March 2005

THE MASTER OF MASTERS: MISTAKEN MYSTIC OSHO!!!

Like an Ocean his wisdom spread,
Whether it be Tantra, Tao or Talmud,
Beyond our consciousness could ever hold,
Fulfilling Krishna, Buddha and Christhood,
To its highest peak we could ever read!

Beyond all knowledge his wisdom hold,
Out-shining all great scriptures too old,
Uniting East and West into his fold,
Beckoning mankind unto his field,
Turning the base metals into gold!

Silence, the only sacred method he used,
Unifying yin and yang in you to behold,
Bursting of unconditional love ever told,
Unto that Ocean of love you're drowned,
By that mystical power you're stunned!

What a dangerous man you have loved,
Your past and future got utterly destroyed,
Now you know not your beginning and end,
Living to the present dropping your useless mind,
Dancing to his tunes never to be disturbed!

Most misunderstood man ever fought,
Against the pope, priest and pandit,
Exposing their evil ways to exploit,
The innocence of mankind utterly lost,
Until that mistaken mystic shall ever last!

Alas, he was too early to visit this world,
Lost to the fury of wars and wound,
Spitting blood of fanatic religious hatred,
A day shall come true to his no-mind,
Where compassion shall be the rule of the God!

Line of control shall lose its role,
Religious fundamentalism shall fail to rule,
Making our mother Earth good to prevail,
Sharing each other's joy and frail,
Celebrating in the name of love so eternal!

Osho shall then descend to make his dream true,
Fulfilling in us his unwritten love so true,
Dancing to our beats of music so divine,
Embracing us together in his cosmic abode,
Cracking the worst sexy jokes with a naughty smile!

26th August 2004

THE SOUND OF SILENCE

Amongst the debris people pathetically searched,

For lives which Tsunami waves had snatched,

Day in and day out stinking bodies they buried,

Where all their belongings too never got spared,

Except animals, birds and trees were saved,

Upon this tragic spell which nature has cursed!

Out of fury they heard a cry so shrill,

A baby amongst ruins where dust fill,

Which the killer waves failed to kill,

Upon the grace of some divine spell,

Beyond all reasons happen such miracle!

Workers of missions ran to its rescue,

Nuns of churches got a strong clue,

Even the Mullas joined this queue,

To possess this fragile body full of hue,

And to let the claim of their religion, so true!

Nobody listened to the baby's hue and cry,
All were bothered of their claim to try,
A babe to the caste and creed they ply,
Police lashed the lathi in the air to fly,
The mob so violent in their religious sly!

The baby wept and wept to quench its thirst,
All were too busy serving their own creed to best,
And before the judge could read his verdict,
The baby became silent to be laid to rest,
When the sound of silent waves still suspect!!!

11th March 2005

A TRIBUTE – IN MEMORIUM

I have lost a good friend, simple and humble,

A co-traveller in this journey, spiritual and helpful,

Whose hands that rocked my destiny's cradle,

Unto his prayerful heart I always want to cuddle;

An Oak tree of love, so unconditional,

Shedding its grace very purposeful,

Yet his tears and silence were unbearable,

O God!, tell me now, am I left all alone, single?

24th January 2004

TWILIGHT

O, Red Sun! before you go,

Remove all my thoughts to go,

Make my mind completely empty so,

It has no past – n – future to know,

Shining in the present, here now,

The only energy too sure, to show!

10th October 2004

UNIVERSAL LOVE

When the sun plays hide 'n' seek with Earth in love,
Rain sprouts out joyously drenching her womb to fertile,
Organisms sprout out henceforth merrily so alive,
Making his beloved planet a heaven for romance,
Where unconditional love blossoms to life so divine!

Earth always looks up praying sun to grace,
Singing love songs glorifying him in praise,
Meditating upon his supreme splendour surprise,
For his radiant power to illuminate all souls,
Empowering wisdom in their hearts to rise!

His universal love shower upon her lives,
Whether they're of any caste, creed or class,
Without any prejudice to shower his grace,
Not out of any religious dogmas and scriptures,
Unto that universal law of love he follows!

Love is his religion and light is his commandment,
For all living beings to survive on his beloved planet,
His energy runs through every living habitat,
Whether it be in darkness or eternal light,
At all times you're under his divine bliss so bright!

Sun is the only living God we see by our eyes,
Only his music of radiance we hear by our ears,
Only his energy of power we feel by our souls,
Unto his divine illumination we all step to dance,
Yet, mankind wages all wars to separate us!

Star wars are mankind's greatest thankless prize,
Mass destructions being its only highest price,
Thus universal energy received from this star of bliss,
Is returned to destroy the stars of all milky ways,
A ruthless way to show our human ingratitudes!

For such atrocities never Sun got wedded to Earth,
To create such monstrous beasts of cruel death,
Destroying all their creations of eternal wealth,
Upon his beloved planet for evolutionary growth,
Taking consciousness unto the highest realms of Truth!

23rd June 2005

UNTO DEATH LET'S LOVE!

Death, the greatest mystery of life,

Love, the only best choice,

Between life and death to be alive,

Life being the starting base,

Death being the highest peak to rise,

And love strides its crescendo at ease!

Science experiments life to create knowledge,

It is of the head to bother and confuse,

All explores love for the heart to care,

Where compassion blossoms to inspires,

To, meditation explodes death to the care,

Shattering all bondages of life to flee!

Life flies unto the wings of love,

Zooming to death, the door of divine,

With death life disappears still alive,

Where the soul inverse in peace,

To the tunes of a mystical fate,

When the mystic open the heavenly gate!!!

10th April 2005

VEDA VYASA CHINMAYANANDA

Chinmaya evolves from the mist of Shankaracharya,
The most treasured pearls of Veda Vyasa,
Foaming like Ganga from the Himalaya,
The great wisdom of Vedanta,
Blessing down trodden souls of Kali yuga!

Twice blessed by the sages of India,
Tapovan Maharaj and Swami Shivananda,
His Geetha Yagna inspires in us the Jyana yoga,
His Chinmaya Vidyalaya teaches us the Karma yoga,
While Chinmaya Mission propagates the Bhakti yoga!

With this Trishul he invokes the Trimurthi,
To awaken us from the desires of our sensory body,
Cleansing our soul to be Karma yogi,
Full of action and power of inner energy,
Praising Krishna to bring back the lost glory!

27th August 2004

WHY LOVE SO PAINFUL?

Why love so painful,
Though it is so powerful,
Unto the God it is equal,
Kids handle it so playful,
Yet man finds it too awful!

Out of love the newborn yells,
To announce the world where he dwells,
Even the mother sheds her tears,
Unto that painful act of love, she sweats,
Over the cradle of mankind which she rocks!

In search of the beloved, it leaves the mom,
Love's greatest fury, yet all keep mum,
To nestle a family of love so firm,
Perhaps the way of nature for love to confirm,
For all our ego burns unto its flame!

Melting of ego is the pain so horrible,
Breaking the bondage of relationship so terrible,
Like the plant erupting out its seed so credible,
Thus the shell of ego ruptures for the love to be flightful,
Seeking its freedom of destiny so truthful!

When the ego dies, love abides,
Death is the door to the divine bliss,
To love is to die to all our egos,
A meditation where the lover dies,
Alive again in the Beloved's hands,
To unfold the secrets of life's mysteries!!!

9th April 2005

WHY ME ....OH LORD!

I am now dying to the past,
Misery, not of my doing,
I am now dying to the future,
Anxiety, not of my craving,
Unto this boring life I strive,
Only to support my sibling!

Guts to suicide, I do not have any,
Cruelty to murder, scares me to worry,
With compassion of heart, madly I hurry,
Like a sailless boat, my life ferry,
Scattering my dreams like a flurry!

To such a life so desperate,
Futility of wealth and kins separate,
The bondage of marriage disintegrate,
Immorality and untruthfulness speculate,
My life depress emotionally to frustrate,
With no mistake of mine, I articulate!

Why me, Oh Lord, for all this tragedy?

30th March 2002

WHY DO OUR PRAYERS GO UNANSWERED?

Our prayers always go unanswered,
Because they were what we wanted,
Unfortunately not what we needed,
And nature has got for our need,
But nothing for our mere greed,
Mostly we pray for the desired,
But she returns what we deserved,
Benevolence is not for the begged,
Benediction is only for the blessed,
The miracles of the good deed,
Not praying in return for any reward,
Hence secret of prayers got resolved!

10th October 2009

A CANDLE IN THE WIND!

Knowledge should liberate the past socially,
Of religious theology and political ideology,
To cleanse the mind of its psychology,
The conflicting world of its philosophy,
Of making some places, books and men holy,
To take mankind for a ride superstitiously!

Enough is enough by its conditioning,
The mind for many generations running,
Without any goal of mutual loving,
Pitted against every religion fiercely fighting,
To be superior to the other causing,
Damages in the consciousness not maturing!

There are no gurus ever blessed,
No doctrines holier ever scripted,
No temples sacred ever sculptured,
All are equal in the eyes of our Beloved,
Nature's great gifts ever created,
For the sake of universal brotherhood!

13th October 2009

DIWALI LAMPS

"Let the Diwali lamps burn bright,
To remove the darkness out of sight,
The universal compassion unto light,
To make this earth a better habitat,
Where positive energy showers in might,
Taking every individual to the highest,
Realms of consciousness of Truth and Trust!"

17th October 2009

HARE KRISHNA!

Thus spake Krishna in Bhagwad Geetha,

Cycle of causes and effects of our karma,
The sacredness of Nishkama karma:
Ma phaleshu kadachanna – Selfless action with fruitless saga,
The highest wisdom of Moksha.
Hare Krishna, Hare Krishna,
Krishna, Krishna, Hare Hare !!!

12th November 2009

"ENTRUSTING MY CHILD WITH YOU"

By taking the hands of my child,

Make her life so fulfilled.

By tying the knot of wedded,

Make her life so sacred.

By bringing her unto your fold,

Remove all her tears shed.

By following a new path to stride,

Remove all her dreams failed.

By living with her as a friend,

Let her dance to the tunes of your sound.

For being the mother of your child,

Invoke the blessings of the God!

And at last if your life is well made,

Pray my soul forever is well laid!

1st August 2010

SATHYAM * SHIVAM * SUNDARAM * SHAKTAM * SHANKARAM

Eshwaram is Sathyam of the Cosmic Energy,
Sathyam is Shivam of the Static Energy,
God is Truth and it is God Universally!

Shivam is Sundaram, the cosmic beauty,
Sundaram is Shakti, the Kinetic energy,
The Manifestation of Mother Nature globally!

Shakti is awakened by Shankaram Theory,
Through the holy verses of Soundarya Lahari,
Initiated by Chakram, Yantram of Divinity!

By the Golden mean ratio of Mahameru Truly,
Blossoming of Cosmic Vibrant Radiance Blissfully,
Through Nirvana Shathakam Peacefully and Spiritually!

For our Transcendence & Transformation soulfully,
Unto the highest realms of Truth eternally,
Tantra is the secret of secrets holistically!

For Salvation and Liberation of our life happily,
Merging with Super Consciousness Intuitively,
The purpose of this deadly life Ultimately!

Chidananda Rupam, Shivoham! Shivoham!!
Sathyam Jnanam Anantham Brahmam!!!

1st August 2010

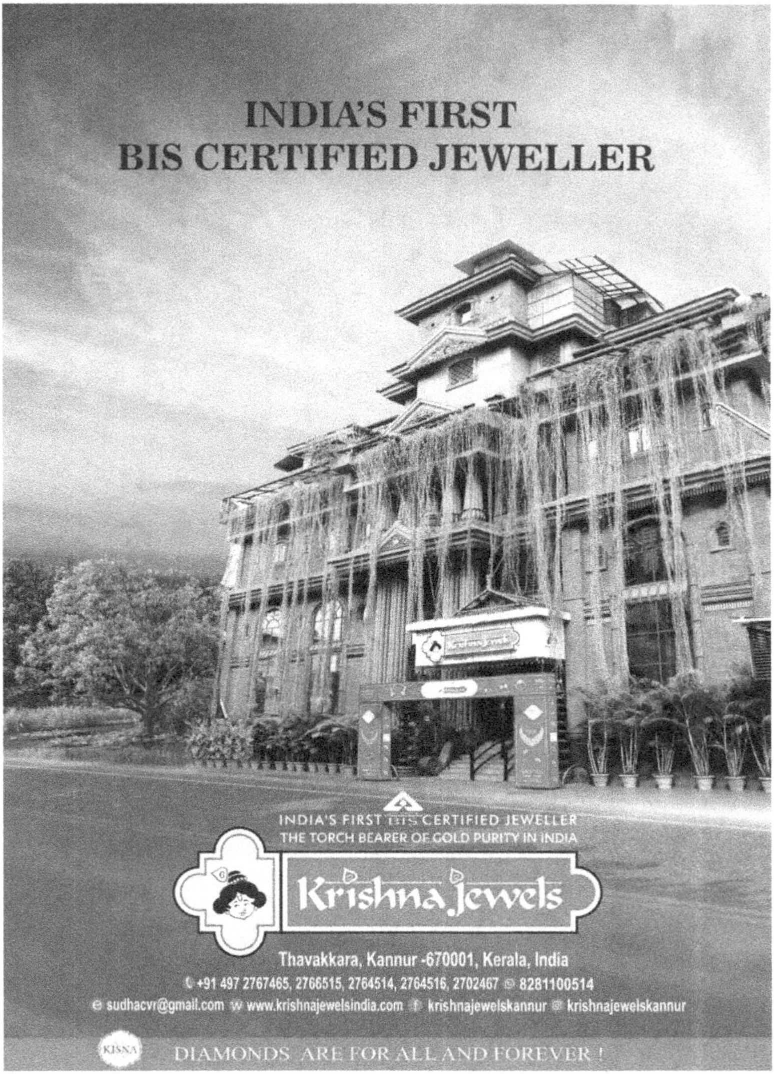
INDIA'S FIRST
BIS CERTIFIED JEWELLER
INDIA'S FIRST BIS CERTIFIED JEWELLER
THE TORCH BEARER OF GOLD PURITY IN INDIA
Krishna Jewels
Thavakkara, Kannur -670001, Kerala, India
+91 497 2767465, 2766515, 2764514, 2764516, 2702467 8281100514
sudhacvr@gmail.com www.krishnajewelsindia.com krishnajewelskannur krishnajewelskannur
KISNA
DIAMONDS ARE FOR ALL AND FOREVER !

Shivoham Spiritual Wellness Centre
Krishna Beach Resort, Palliyamoola, Kannur Presents:

LIFESTYLE HEALTH PACKAGE
FOR THE REJUVENATION OF BODY, MIND AND SOUL

For Booking: 📞 7558887704   ☎ 0497 2715888

reservation@kbrkannur.com / krishnabeachresort.knr@gmail.com / om@kbrkannur.com 7558887704 www.kbrkannur.com

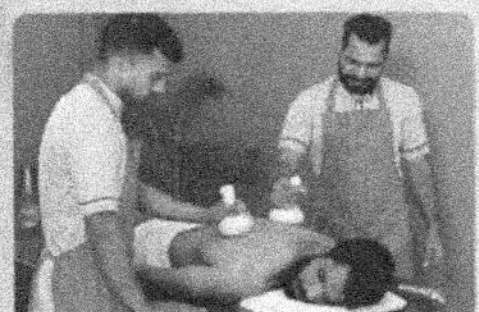
AYURVEDA MASSAGE

KALARIPAYATTU

YOGA

ENHANCE YOUR HAPPY HORMONES SUCH AS DOPAMINE,
SEROTONIN, OXYTOCIN ENDORPHIN AND MELATONIN THROUGH AYUR CARE,
YOGA, KALARIPAYATTU AND TANTRA.

We Care Spiritual Wellness Tourism

Thavakkara, Kannur -670001, Kerala, India
+91 497 2767465, 2766515, 2764514, 2754516, 2702467 8281100514
sudhacvr@gmail.com www.krishnajewelsindia.com
krishnajewelskannur krishnajewelskannur

Payyambalam - Palliyamoola Kannur-8 Kerala India
0497 2715888 7558887704
reservations@kbrkannur.com, krishnabeachresort.knr@gmail.com
om@kbrkannur.com www.kbrkannur.com krishnabeachresort

Buy Jewellery at Krishna Jewels to win a Honeymoon suite at Krishna Beach Resort.

A Spiritual Ecstasy of Tantric Creativity!

With the blessings of **Jagadguru Sri Adi Shankaracharya**

ॐ Shiva - Shakti Pendant

Available in Gold, Silver & Copper
for positive energy - Peace & Prosperity.

Energy report on the ॐ Shiva - Shakti Pendant of Maharishi University
of Spirituality Research Team, Goa, dt.11.9.2023

1. **Universal Aura Scan reading:** Positive aura of 9.84 metres in copper.
2. **Subtle analysis:** The pendant emits positive energy. It is **SATTVIK**.
3. **Anubuti (Spiritual experience):** While Looking at the pendant, calmness
   was felt and the pace of breathing became low. Pleasantness is felt.

Maharishi Adhyatma Vishwavidyalay, Goa
www.spiritual.university | e-mail: mav.research2014@gmail.com | Call: 9561574972, 8451006060